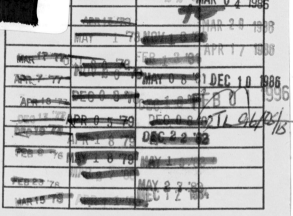
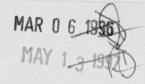

Franz Kafka

by WALTER H. SOKEL

Columbia University Press

NEW YORK *&* LONDON

COLUMBIA ESSAYS ON MODERN WRITERS is a series of critical studies of English, Continental, and other writers whose works are of contemporary artistic and intellectual significance.

Editor: William York Tindall

Advisory Editors
Jacques Barzun   W. T. H. Jackson   Joseph A. Mazzeo   Justin O'Brien

Franz Kafka is Number 19 of the series

WALTER H. SOKEL is Professor of German at Stanford University. He is the author of several books: *The Writer in Extremis: Expressionism in Twentieth-Century German Literature. Franz Kafka: Tragik und Ironie. An Anthology of German Expressionist Drama.*

ISBN 0-231-02751-6
Library of Congress Catalog Card Number: 66-26005
Printed in the United States of America

Franz Kafka

Franz Kafka was born on July 3, 1883, the only surviving son of Hermann Kafka, a self-made businessman and prosperous shopkeeper in the heart of the "Old Town" of Prague. The figure of his father loomed enormous in the emotional life of the son. Kafka saw in his vigorous father the example of life "dans le vrai", Flaubert's phrase which Kafka applied to a way of life from which his own nature excluded him.

The works published by Kafka during his life do not comprise more than a single volume in the six-volume edition of his works, edited and published posthumously by his close friend Max Brod. These six volumes consist of three major novels, two volumes of stories, and a volume of miscellaneous pieces, including his very significant aphorisms. Kafka's diaries (1910-1923), his letters published by Max Brod, and the letters to Milena Jesenská-Pollak, his Czech woman friend and translator, published by Willy Haas, form three additional volumes. It is important to realize that Kafka himself neither completed nor edited the bulk of his writings, including his three great novels, *Amerika*, *The Trial*, and *The Castle*, all of which are fragments. The only narratives of normal story length he completed were those published during his life. These must consequently occupy a privileged position in any critical concern with Kafka's work.

Kafka's work can be called a spiritual autobiography clothed in metaphoric disguise. In a diary entry of August 6, 1914,

[3]

Kafka noted that his sense for the presentation of his "dream-like inner life" had stunted all his other interests and talents and had become the only quality that could afford him full satisfaction. Indeed, the oneiric character of Kafka's writings strikes every reader. Their enigmatic suggestiveness is their most pronounced feature. They are like dreams in that they compel interpretation but seem to withhold the key. Sometimes his stories did grow out of dreams, and the dreams Kafka frequently relates in his diaries show a striking resemblance to his stories. Yet his writings differ profoundly from those of the surrealists who jotted down their dreams in automatic writing. Unlike theirs, Kafka's narratives are thoroughly disciplined. They are by no means simple copies of dreams; rather they are structured analogous to dreams in some essential respects.

One of these characteristics is the peculiar relationship of Kafka's narratives to metaphor. His stories tend to present enactments of metaphors buried in language, not only in the German language in which he wrote but also in the universal symbolism of prerational thought. Basic metaphors by which prescientific language expresses experiences, attitudes, and relationships become event in Kafka's tales. He re-instates, or re-creates, the pictorial expressiveness which the original metaphor, frozen in a cliché or idiom, once conveyed. Thus Kafka's writing conforms to or repeats the activity of the dreaming mind. As Freud has shown in his *Interpretation of Dreams*, a work with which Kafka was familiar, dreams speak in the pictorial language speech once was. They take the metaphors hidden in speech literally and act them out as visualized events.

A few examples might help to clarify the preceding remarks. A decisive and profound experience is said to "leave a mark"; a lasting memory is "engraved" on one. Kafka's *The Penal Colony* depicts both metaphors as physical happenings. The penal machine slowly kills the condemned prisoner by literally engraving (German: *einkerben*) on his flesh the law he transgressed. He dies, in fact, of his remembering this lesson; "the mark left" by the law kills him. German usage applies the term *Ungeziefer* (vermin) to persons considered low and contemptible, even as our usage of "cockroach" describes a person deemed a spineless and miserable character. The traveling salesman Gregor Samsa, in Kafka's *The Metamorphosis*, is "like a cockroach" because of his spineless and abject behavior and parasitic wishes. However, Kafka drops the word "like" and has the metaphor become reality when Gregor Samsa wakes up finding himself turned into a giant vermin. With this metamorphosis, Kafka reverses the original act of metamorphosis carried out by thought when it forms metaphor; for metaphor is always "metamorphosis." Kafka transforms metaphor back into his fictional reality, and this counter-metamorphosis becomes the starting point of his tale. German usage calls a sexually indecent and obscene character a "pig" or "swine" (*Schwein*). In Kafka's tale, "A Country Doctor," the groom who assaults the doctor's maid walks out of the doctor's pigsty.

Kafka's narratives do not stop with reactivating single metaphors. They connect organically the enactment of one metaphor with the enactments of others; together these establish a narrative development. "A Country Doctor" will serve as an example.

The swinish groom stands in a fateful relation to the protagonist of the story, the country doctor, through whose consciousness alone we witness the events. The doctor had lived next to his maid, Rose, without noticing her as a woman. As soon as she presents herself to him as desirable, the groom steps out of the doctor's *unused* * pigsty and seeks to rape her. The unused pigsty belongs to the doctor; it is, in the words of

* The original text uses the German word for "unused"—*unbenützt*—which the English translation renders as "uninhabited."

[5]

the story, "his own." The groom is, then, literally a dweller of the doctor's forgotten lower depths. He embodies the doctor's unused sex drive in a strikingly literal way. The doctor's consciousness does not acknowledge his responsibility for the event he himself has called forth when he kicked the door of the pigsty open "absent-mindedly" and thus released the groom. The sudden emergence of the "filthy" contents of the doctor's depths—the unacknowledged component of his self—now overpowers his humanity and makes the girl a prey of bestial desire. In Kafka's stories, acts and omissions reveal what consciousness hides from itself. Not consciousness—the explicit comments of the story—but the narrated events show the true meaning of Kafka's tale. "A Country Doctor" begins with a call of the night bell summoning the doctor to a patient. However, his horse had died from overexertion and he cannot follow his call. In his dilemma, he calls "absent-mindedly" * (that is, unconsciously) on his forgotten pigsty, releasing the swinish groom and a team of "unearthly horses" and allows the groom to take the girl. Contrary to his verbal protestations, the doctor does in fact leave Rose behind with the groom. She is the price for the groom's aid.

Images and plot of this tale enable us to see Kafka's works as pieces of an autobiography in metaphoric disguise. The "call" of the night bell is a translation into sensory terms of Kafka's "call" to literature, which he understood as an art of healing and self-preservation, a "doctor's" art. Writing for Kafka was night work in two respects: literally, because he had no time for it during the day; figuratively, because he had to delve into the nocturnal regions of his mind, the representation of which he called his fatal talent. The death of the horse shows that no normal and natural way is available for trans-

* The original text uses the German word for "absent-mindedly"— *zerstreut*—which the English translation renders as "confused."

porting the self to its calling. As the doctor finds his self in absent-mindedness, Kafka notes that he had done his best writing when all rational control was lifted. In one night, with "an outpouring of his soul," he wrote *The Judgment*, which remained his favorite work and model of all others.

"A Country Doctor" presents in the hieroglyphic language of dreams a clear and exact presentation of Kafka's inspirational process and the problems it posed for his life. In a revealing letter to Max Brod, in 1922, he calls his writing a "descent to the dark powers, an unchaining of spirits whose natural state it is to be bound servants." The description fits the groom of "A Country Doctor," who, instead of serving the self, expels it and takes over its vacated house. In that same letter to Brod, Kafka says that, in order to devote himself to literature, the writer must sacrifice fulfillment in life. The "unearthly horses" of inspiration, called forth from the unsavory depths, transport the doctor away from life, woman, and home. He is shown literally "carried away," "in the transport" of inspiration, since his unearthly team of horses proceeds without his conscious will and carries him off instantaneously and miraculously to his vocational destination. This destination is an existential encounter, symbolized by his being undressed and put in the same bed with his sick childhood self, the boy patient to whom he has been called.

The two houses pictorialize the two poles of the doctor's existence. In his own house, the house of the self, the doctor abandoned the possibility of erotic fulfillment; in the other house, the house of the patient, he is to dedicate himself to his art, which is the confrontation with the congenital wound of mortality. The hero's ambivalence is such that he cannot be content at either pole. At home he sacrifices the girl to his mission; but at his destination he regrets the price he has paid and wants to return. His split existence, his inability to choose,

[7]

becomes pure image in the doctor's final condition. He is shown riding aimlessly between the houses; the distance between them has become infinite, and he cannot stay at either place.

"A Country Doctor" became the title story of a volume of Kafka's short pieces published in 1919 and dedicated to his father, which makes the importance Kafka attached to this particular work quite evident. The detailed examination of its plot and images has enabled us to understand the allegorical principle informing Kafka's writings. His images are pictorial translations of over-riding personal concerns in which personal meaning acquires universal significance.

Any individual work by Kafka may baffle the reader when considered in isolation. If examined within the context of Kafka's other works and personal documents, the nature and meaning of his images become clear. The individual work will then appear as a variation of a single theme—the inner autobiography of the author—and a step in its development. Each work is aesthetically self-sufficient and, if completed and published by Kafka himself, a complete and satisfying statement of one approach to the master theme.

There is, nevertheless, a difference in the degree of transparency Kafka's images possess in different works. The central images of his long narratives—Gregor Samsa's bug form, the Court in *The Trial*, the Castle in the late novel of that name— are more opaque and denser than the symbols of his shorter pieces. The reason is that the central images of the long works have a variety of functions and meanings. Indeed, they unite mutually contradictory meanings and functions.

Gregor Samsa's metamorphosis, for instance, expresses a number of contradictory tendencies in the single image of the giant bug. Gregor's transformation gives shape to his wish to abandon responsibility as breadwinner and supporter of his family, and thereby returns Gregor's father to his former position as head of the household. At the same time, however, his metamorphosis embodies Gregor's opposite wish to avenge himself on his family's parasitism by turning parasite himself. In the former case the metamorphosis functions as submission; in the latter as aggression and rebellion. The empirical impossibility of Gregor's form of existence serves as objective correlative of his spiritual and psychic contradictoriness.

There are two further factors which make the structure of Kafka's stories analogous to the structure of dreams: unitary perspective and tension between a manifest content and a latent truth.

In fiction, ordinarily, the community of author and reader stands as objective reality outside and above the points of view of the characters and forms a "true" frame of reference. The traditional story-teller or novelist maintains this division by one or both of these devices: he switches the point of view from one character to another, and thus enables us to enjoy a relative omniscience since we can look into all minds of the story, which none of the characters can; or he keeps his own perspective separate, looks into his characters, and comments upon their thoughts and actions. These conventions are absent in Kafka's fiction. His stories know only a single point of view, that of the protagonist. Even in his third-person narratives—and his major works are all third-person narratives—objects, scenes, and persons are seen by us only through the protagonist's eyes. An example from *The Trial* may illustrate the means by which Kafka replaces independent authorial comment by his protagonist's interpretation of the action.

The reaction of the Examining Magistrate to a demagogic speech by the defendant Josef K. is described as follows: "The Examining Magistrate kept fidgeting on his chair with embarrassment *or* impatience." [Italics mine.] The word "or" shows Kafka's radical deviation from the conventional method of narration. Instead of giving us a single authoritative explanation, the author states his ignorance of his fictional world. He blocks and prevents the traditional communication of author to reader "over the head of the character." With this, Kafka achieves the most fundamental realism and removes the last vestiges of the author's presence as an independent, visible personality, thereby fulfilling Flaubert's ideal of an author who is as omnipresent and invisible as God is in his creation. However, he goes further than Flaubert by also taking away the reader's fictional superiority over the protagonist. Together with the protagonist, the reader is thrown into the basic condition of every individual man: He stays imprisoned in the solitary confinement of a limited and subjective consciousness that can only infer, but can never know, the external world. Normally, we accept on trust "the truth" of our fellow man's feelings and motivations. The Kafka hero lacks this *a priori* trust; or if he does start out with it, events take it away from him or, at least, from the reader. This loss of basic trust or faith in the predictability of the world around the protagonist explains the peculiar effect of Kafka's fiction.

For reasons which we shall examine later, Kafka's hero must defend and assert himself, or else be lost. Josef K.'s alternative interpretation, for instance, of the Examining Magistrate's fidgeting results from his need to calculate the effect of his speech. If it was embarrassment that made the Magistrate fidget, Josef K. has scored a victory. If, on the other hand, the Magistrate moved from impatience, K.'s speech has heightened the threat to himself. The fictional reality presented by Kafka is either threat or promise to the protagonist and wholly related to his fears, wishes, and hopes. Therefore, there can be no presentation of facts in Kafka that is not, at the same time, interpretation. The situation of Kafka's pro-

[10]

tagonist reflects the fundamental insecurity of man's condition as prisoner of his brain.

All aspects of Kafka's narrative form, from individual word and sentence to plot structure and thought, express this fundamental uncertainty of his protagonists, and it is this form that infects the reader and grips him with foreboding. Kafka's vocabulary is one of inference and conjecture. Favorite words are "apparently," "ostensibly," "maybe," "actually." Kafka prefers "it seems" to "it is." His sentences often consist of two clauses: the first states a fact or a guess; the second qualifies, questions, negates it. The conjunction "but" is, therefore, most characteristic of Kafka's thought structure. The frequent use of "even if" clauses expresses the tendency to cancel expectations and refute inferences. Terminal certainty there is in Kafka, but usually of a negative kind, identical with death or final despair. The fragmentary form of most works not ending with the protagonist's death attests to the inability of arriving at certainty.

More than most writers, Kafka favors the subjunctive. The only bridge between the protagonist and his environment is surmise. Kafka's subjunctive acts as the grammatical correlative of the structural device called *anagnorisis*—"discovery"— in Aristotle's *Poetics*. It is the hero's surprise at the unexpected turns of events. However, the anagnorisis in classical tragedy leads to insight on the part of both hero and audience. Its main function in Kafka is to reveal the discrepancy between the protagonist's consciousness and the truth underlying the story.

We have just shown that the protagonist's solipsistic perspective, through which we experience the narrative, does not allow us to speak of authorial truth in Kafka's work. Yet there is an objective and verifiable authorial truth in most of his writings. It is obliquely smuggled in against the consciousness of the protagonist. In the contradiction between the reader's

[11]

perspective, as given him by the protagonist, and the hidden truth of the work lies the fundamental concern of Kafka's art, the basis of its structure, and the secret of its unsettling effect.

Those who think that the protagonist's perspective is the whole of Kafka are victims of the subtle deception perpetrated by it. In the two K. novels and several of the longer narratives, the protagonist's motivation is to hide the truth either from himself or from the world, including the reader. However, in most of Kafka's works the truth becomes known. The protagonist's perspective, to be sure, operates for the purpose of blocking access to and comprehension of the truth, but the truth of the story emerges through the defeat of the protagonist's consciousness. In one of his aphorisms, Kafka defined truth as the light reflected upon the retreating grimace (of falsehood) and art as the condition of being dazzled by that light. This aphorism supplies the key to Kafka's poetics, always implicit in his works. The annihilation or refutation suffered by Kafka's protagonist, bearer of the lie, becomes the negative revelation of truth.

This structural principle of Kafka's narratives explains the profound difference between Kafka's method and the stream-of-consciousness technique. The latter assumes the identity of consciousness and truth. It reveals character and, with character, the truth of the narrative. It operates within the framework of psychology. In Kafka's narratives, on the contrary, consciousness hides truth. Therefore, Kafka has to transcend psychology. His concern is not the mechanism of self, but its moral and spiritual justification. In order to express this concern, he must unmask the mechanism, and in doing that he reveals a great deal about it. Kafka is a master in uncovering the subtle workings of rationalization, subterfuge, self-deception. But for Kafka this unmasking is not the end of his art.

[12]

The end is always the revelation of truth in the defeat of the self.

All of Kafka's works deal with this relationship in one of three ways. Each of them corresponds to one of the three distinct phases of development in his mature writings. In the first phase of his maturity (1912–1914) the protagonist represses his inner truth, but his truth erupts in a catastrophe—accuses, judges, and annihilates him. This is the phase of the punitive fantasies, the powerful tales of punishment and death which are Kafka's most dramatic and popular—*The Judgment* and *The Metamorphosis,* *The Trial*, with important modifications, and partially *The Penal Colony*. To all of these, *Amerika* forms an "innocent" and "utopian" counterpart. The second phase (1914–1917) begins with *The Penal Colony* and continues with the short parabolic pieces of the *Country Doctor* volume which includes the "legend," "Before the Law," and "A Report to an Academy." In this phase a detached perspective views and contemplates a paradoxical discrepancy between self and truth.

The final phase (1920–1924) is Kafka's greatest and most profound. It comprises the four stories of the *Hunger Artist* volume, the lengthy fragments, "Investigations of a Dog" and "The Burrow," and the long fragmentary novel, *The Castle*. In the three most important works of that phase—"A Hunger Artist," "Josephine the Singer, or the Mouse Folk," and *The Castle*—Kafka presents the protagonist's deception of the world, perpetrated by his desperate need to create and fulfill his existence.

The punitive fantasies form the foundation for all phases of Kafka's maturity. With *The Judgment*, he said, he had achieved his "breakthrough" to his own proper form of expression. We shall, therefore, deal with the punitive fantasies in greater detail than with the two subsequent phases.

[13]

The alienation of the protagonist from his true self forms the structural basis of Kafka's punitive fantasies. These fantasies are adumbrated in the early fragment, "Wedding Preparations in the Country." Here the hero—Raban, cryptographic forerunner of Samsa and disguise for Kafka—dreams of literally splitting his self in order to evade visits to his fiancée in the country and other burdensome involvements. His true self, transformed into a giant beetle, would stay in bed, while the unreal image of his body, his façade, would go into the world to represent Raban in the performance of necessary duties. This façade would be a slave, utterly dependent upon the commands of the powerful dehumanized self at home. This bug-like true self corresponds to the bachelor self of other early writings and diary entries of Kafka. Raban's façade body, on the other hand, burdened with the task of conducting his engagement, corresponds to the engaged young men who appear in Kafka's juvenilia.

This split prefigures the structure of Kafka's punitive fantasies, with one essential qualification. What the early work presents as a conscious wish becomes in the punitive fantasies a strange destiny, seemingly imposed upon the protagonist from outside and eluding his conscious understanding. What in the early work is a split between façade body and true self reappears in Kafka's mature work as a contradiction between consciousness and truth.

Kafka's punitive fantasies—leaving *The Penal Colony* out of account for the present—are related to Raban's wish dream in the following manner. The façade tries to make itself independent of the true self by seeking to repress it. Punishment acts as a recall to the self. Having tried to emancipate itself, the façade is arrested, battered, and dissolved.

With the element of repression, time is introduced as a structural element into the split. What was in Raban's wish-

dream an open horizontal coexistence of two halves now becomes a vertical division of two layers; a visible surface layer
stands on top of a deeper, submerged layer which the surface
tries to "cover up." The protagonist's true self—essentially his
childhood self—lies submerged, but erupts one day in a strange
guise, arrests him in his course of self-emancipation, involves
him ever more deeply and catastrophically in his unacknowledged truth, and destroys him.

Arrest is central fact and symbol in *The Trial,* Kafka's long-
est and most ambitious tale of punishment. The German word
for arrest, *Verhaftung,* carries the additional meaning of entanglement and fatal attachment. In this basic meaning, *Verhaftung* is the theme of all the punitive fantasies. The protagonist's condition of attachment to his childhood self has been
repressed and put out of mind, but never truly overcome. The
act or happening of his being arrested (literally stopped in his
advance) by a catastrophic event is the emergence of the invisible condition of entanglement which had persisted in him
all along. Estranged from his conscious intentions, however,
his true condition, when it does erupt, manifests itself in an
unrecognizable disguise.

The turning point and "breakthrough" to his mature form,
which Kafka considered his first punitive fantasy, *The Judgment,* to be, lie in two factors: the introduction of the father
figure as the authoritative and effective voice of truth; and the
consistent shift of perspective to the façade layer of the split.
Kafka's juvenilia had been uncertain about perspective and,
therefore, hampered by a subjectivism unable to push through
to an effective objectification of the themes and problems he
sought to express. In Raban's wish-dream the authentic consciousness of the story looks upon the façade, and what the
reader obtains is an unformed reverie. The revolution of *The
Judgment* consisted in the reversal of the perspective. Kafka

[15]

made the façade the consciousness of the story, whereby he achieved the powerful alienation effect that we associate with his art. He was able to present consciousness estranged from itself in a way that involved the reader directly, from within the narration, instead of letting him look in from outside.

Since Gregor Samsa's true self manifests itself in the bug form of Raban's wish-dream, *The Metamorphosis* offers an obvious basis for comparison, which can enable us to assess the narrative method and meaning of the punitive fantasies.

In both stories the transformed self is the true self. However, Samsa's transformation, unlike Raban's, emerges from his night dreams and becomes reality. The text clearly refers to the subconscious origin of the metamorphosis by explicitly mentioning that Gregor finds himself changed into vermin upon awakening from "restless dreams." In the early version the transformation expresses what Raban wants to be. In the mature version truth is not what the self wants to be, but what it is. In the early version truth and consciousness are identical; in the mature version they are not. Furthermore, while both versions agree on the retrograde and inhuman nature of the true self, they differ as to the presentation of the façade. Whereas Raban's façade is an unreal body, Samsa's façade is an evasive mind. It is consciousness finding itself imprisoned in a truth it cannot face. In the mature work the split between façade and true self is a discrepancy between a devious human mind and a non-human body.

Gregor pretends to himself, and tries to pretend to others, that his metamorphosis is a temporary inconvenience. At the same time he feels a vague uneasiness and sense of guilt for having reneged on his obligations toward his family. His stream of memories reveals that, prior to his metamorphosis, Gregor had indeed thought of giving up his distasteful job. However, for the sake of his family, who depended upon his income, he had had to inhibit this wish, and it has received no further attention from him. Seen with this sequence in mind, Gregor's metamorphosis appears and functions as the oblique fulfillment of a wish that had to be repressed. However, Gregor emphatically wards off such suspicions, claiming that he is "still around" and does not intend to abandon his responsibility. This is the manifest content of the story, which is identical with the protagonist's perspective. The reader tends to accept this content at face value, since he sees all happenings of the story through the protagonist's perspective, and tends also to make that perspective his own.

However, Gregor's avowal to continue as his family's provider offers a glaring contradiction to his condition. The thought does indeed occur to Gregor that his situation must rule out his professed intention. He allows himself the fleeting wish to be left in peace by his family. This wish accords perfectly with his new bodily state and resurrects his previously inhibited thought of abandoning his duties. His physical change can now be seen as a fulfillment of Gregor's wish for seclusion and irresponsibility; it is the abandonment of his family, in fact, which he has indignantly denied in thought. When Gregor wishes to be left in peace, his consciousness and condition meet harmoniously. However, it is so only for a moment. Immediately thereafter, Gregor's false consciousness—that is, thought inconsistent with condition—"covers up" and takes over once more the manifest content of the story.

In the punitive fantasies the repressed part of the self is identical with its child-like component. In a time now long past, the protagonist enjoyed a harmonious relationship with his origins, his parents and family; the loss of this harmonious past plays a very important part in bringing about the vengeance and punishment he suffers. This is most obvious in *The Judgment*, least so in *The Trial*. Yet even in *The Trial*, the

[17]

hero's attachment to his family functions importantly in his punishment. At one point in the novel, Josef K. feels that only the pressures of his family have so desperately involved him in his strange trial. Josef K.'s mother in particular has a vital function in the structure of the novel. On his birthdays Joseph K. had been in the habit of visiting his mother, whom he had left behind in the country. Being preoccupied with his strenuous career at the bank, he had become estranged from her and had given up his visits. On the third birthday after he had stopped seeing her, the mysterious court visits him to arrest him for an unspecified guilt. His estrangement from his family—indicated also by his annoyance at his uncle, whom he calls "a revenant from the country," and neglect of his cousin—vaguely troubles him. However, like all protagonists of the punitive fantasies, Josef K. easily represses whatever makes him feel uneasy and pays little conscious attention to it.

In all his works Kafka equates truth or objective reality with the family, first in its basic meaning, later in a more and more extended meaning, which became identical with society, stream of the generations, or totality of living things. "The entire community of men and animals," he once termed this total community from which he felt he had defected. It is against this family that he contrasts the self of his protagonists. The representative or spokesman of the family is the father figure.

A close study of the attributes of all representatives of authority in Kafka's entire *opus*, no matter how universalized and abstract, clearly reveals that these derive from the attributes of the fathers in *The Judgment* and *The Metamorphosis*. From *The Judgment* to Kafka's last work, "Josephine," this father figure possesses a power that, however unseen, mysterious, and generalized it becomes, retains a fundamental effectiveness that plays havoc with the assumptions, opinions, and claims of Kafka's protagonist. It is the father figure which proves the hero's consciousness to be illusion.

In Georg Bendemann and Gregor Samsa, heroes of the first two punitive fantasies, Kafka created characters who had tried to rival and succeed their fathers, failed in the attempt, and were horribly punished for it. Indeed, in *The Metamorphosis*, Kafka places his protagonist in a condition in which he literally becomes incomparable to his father by ceasing to belong to the same species.

The father is allied with the submerged pole of his son's divided self. He enforces those tendencies in his son that crave for regression to a child-like existence which finds its radical objectification in Gregor's vermin condition. This form of existence combines the son's self-elimination as a possible rival and threat to the father with self-indulgence in a narcissistic freedom.

The composition of the story makes clear this alliance between the protagonist's father and the son's subconscious self. Each of the three parts into which the story is divided shows an attempt on Gregor's part to break out into the world and reassert himself as a responsible adult human being. Each part ends with his being rebuffed and chased back into his prison room. It is Gregor's father, who, as spokesman of the family, administers the first two of these rebuffs. Thereby, he enforces Gregor's own tendency toward withdrawal and seclusion that he expressed by locking himself in his room and emerging from his dreams as a creature unable to communicate. He acts as the executor of Gregor's own innermost force. In *The Judgment*, Georg Bendemann's father explicitly calls himself "the representative" of Georg's estranged childhood friend, who exerts upon Georg an effect analogous to the force that erupts in Gregor's metamorphosis.

The Judgment shows the son literally "covering up" his

apparently senile father after having put him to bed like a child. On the manifest level he acts from filial solicitude. On the latent level, which, as Georg's reactions later show is the true one, he seeks to bury his father and establish his own position as new head of the household. Georg thinks of himself as a good and dutiful son, and seeing him through his perspective we are inclined to agree with him. Actually, however, he has neglected his father, has allowed him to live in the gloomy back room of the apartment while he himself occupied the sunny front (literally the façade), and has not set foot in his father's room for a very long time. He thinks he has taken his father's place in the family business and prides himself on having greatly improved and reformed it. With his impending marriage, Georg consciously plans to move his father to his new apartment and there, reversing the role of child and parent, "take care of him." But Georg is only deceiving himself. He has not succeeded in keeping his father "covered." His father shouts "No!", throws off his covers, leaps up in bed, and reveals himself in his true stature as the giant and supreme judge in the heart of his son.

Truth is revealed to be the opposite of Georg's imaginings. His father, is not senile, but "still a giant" whose fingertips reach the ceiling. His fiancée, whom he had thought to be so important in his life, matters so little to Georg that she no longer enters his mind. What counts in his soul is not the girl he wanted to marry, but the friend he thought he had long outgrown and had patronized. This friend now grips and "touches his imagination as never before." This friend (whom Kafka in his own analysis of *The Judgment* called the only common bond of father and son) is Georg's last tie to his childhood and represented an existence "after the father's own heart." Georg loses fiancée, business, status, and power, all in one stroke; but inwardly he had never truly possessed them.

[20]

For the only loss that matters to him is the loss of his friend in himself. Having lost him, Georg is lost.

The father's accusations prove the entire content of Georg's consciousness to be error and self-deception. They shatter his false consciousness, his wrong self-estimation, and through this shattered façade they reach to and lay bare Georg's hidden child-like self. By rushing to obey his father's death sentence and execute himself, he becomes again the loving, innocent, and obedient child he had once been. The inner division is gone; the façade is removed; harmony has returned. As Georg climbs over the railing to leap from the bridge, his consciousness of loving his parents is his whole truth. It was this truth that his father had demanded of Georg at the beginning of his cross-examination; Georg had been unable to give it except by destroying the untruth that his life had become.

The guilt of the protagonists of *The Judgment* and *The Metamorphosis* is clearly established. In *The Judgment* Georg's guilt is his defection from father and childhood friend, and the "devilish" lechery with which he utilized woman as his instrument for the repression of his friend and childhood self. His father uses the drastic metaphor accusing Georg of subjugating his friend so that he could "set [his] bottom on him." Georg's guilt above all lies in the unconscious hypocrisy with which he attempted to displace his father while thinking himself a good son. Whether or not we accept the father's harsh judgment as justified is less relevant than the hero's active assent to his death sentence.

Less explicit than *The Judgment* on the verbal level, but equally lucid in poetic terms, *The Metamorphosis* supplies articulated reasons for accusing and condemning its protagonist. Gregor is clearly punished for trying to break out of the "otherness" that he has made his fate. Gregor's sister articulates what amounts to the family's death sentence over him. Her argument is clear and convinces Gregor. If the insect were truly her brother, it would have left them of its own accord. If he had acted according to the inner law that found its visible fulfillment in his ghastly change, he would have continued to withdraw not only from the human form but also from the human community represented by his family. If Gregor had been his true self, he would have gone into ultimate loneliness, and death would have been self-fulfillment. Then his family could have honored his memory. The disgusting monster and parasite is his false self that refuses to die. Instead, it makes forays into the family and seeks to exploit and ruin them. It is this parasitic and hostile self that the sister exposes, judges, and condemns, with uncompromising cruelty.

The sister's judgment in *The Metamorphosis* corresponds to the father's in the earlier story. However, more clearly than there, it is the judgment of the family and life itself that speaks through her. Gregor had withdrawn from the possibility of procreating even before his metamorphosis; he had remained a bachelor who loved to lock himself in when he dreamed. Therefore, the hope for a renewal of the family in the next generation rested entirely with his sister. As the scene after Gregor's death shows, it is through her that the family will continue and the stream of the generations will flow. It is the authority of life itself that judges Gregor through his sister's cruelty.

This clear judgment speaks to him with the voice of his own inner truth. As Georg rushed to execute his father's verdict on himself, Gregor is convinced, more firmly even than his sister, that he must go. Both stories end with statements of inner assent to death. Both protagonists become true sons and truly themselves by dying.

In *The Penal Colony* Kafka systematized the underlying idea of the two earlier punitive fantasies. The penal machine

[24]

produces, in a six-hour process of physical torture and laceration, that assent to death which the judgment of their families produced in Kafka's earlier protagonists. In the later work the father's judgment and family consensus have evolved into the law of a penal system. The Old Commander, who invented and operated the penal machine, constitutes the obvious link between the concrete fathers of *The Judgment* and *The Metamorphosis* and the abstract law and collective, anonymous authorities of *The Trial* and all subsequent works. The colony is the first step in Kafka's extension of the empirical family to the societies, nations, and species with which his later work is concerned.

The Old Commander's verdict is inscribed into the flesh of the condemned prisoner who deciphers it with his wounds. As he recognizes the text of the law on his body, he experiences a union with the paternal will more intimate—because physical—than Georg Bendemann's merely symbolic reunion in suicide with his father's will.

The penal machine does not restore, but creates its victim's true self. Before his arrest the prisoner was not much more than an animal. He lived in an unconscious state, ignorant of the law he violated. His dawning recognition of the sentence, as the machine inscribes it into his skin, creates a comprehensible continuity between act and atonement. By connecting his pain with the law he transgressed, he acquires a destiny that is uniquely his and, at the same time, his inward relationship to a superior will.

The continuity of self produced on the penal rack parallels Kierkegaard's idea of the self. (At the time of the punitive fantasies Kafka called Kierkegaard a "friend." He first became acquainted with Kierkegaard through an anthology entitled *Book of the Judge*, a title spelling out a significant affinity between them.) The authentic self in Kierkegaard is not identi-

[23]

cal with the organism, but with a moral continuity which we create by our choices and actions, and through a special and unique personal relationship to the Absolute. In Kafka's penal system suffering and dying give birth to the same kind of existential self.

Their dying not only restores Kafka's earlier protagonists to the true self of each, but also reconciles them to their families, and through their families, to the world. The sacrifice of Georg's false self re-establishes the harmony of life not in actuality but in principle. Georg's drowning in the river symbolically reunites him with the "stream of life" that proceeds above him in the "unending traffic" over the bridge from which he had leaped to his death.

When, at the beginning of the story, he had looked out upon the bridge, a quiet emptiness, a kind of frozen suspension of life, prevailed. His dying re-animates life. Although, chronologically, only a short time could have passed since the beginning of the action, symbolically a resurrection has taken place. The German word for "traffic"—*Verkehr*—also signifies "intercourse." The word alludes to the sexual and procreative aspect of the "unending" stream released by Georg's death. A remark made by Kafka to Max Brod corroborates the allusion. As he wrote the word *Verkehr* with which he concluded the story, Kafka, according to Brod, had thought of an ejaculation. The end of *The Metamorphosis* is more directly explicit about the sexual and procreative liberation achieved by the hero's voluntary death. Gregor's demise frees his family from the guilt and shame which had become embodied in him. It allows thoughts of the future, of youth, marriage, and new bloom to burst forth. Fittingly, the day of his death is the first day of real spring. Gregor Samsa dies as a scapegoat for humanity, represented by his family. In a letter to Max Brod, Kafka designated the writer a scapegoat for mankind. By taking mankind's sins upon himself and suffering for them, the writer allows mankind to sin in freedom.

The idea of the scapegoat led Kafka to find analogous insights in the anthropological research of his time and in the proto-totalitarian tendencies becoming noticeable in Central Europe, in his day. Both the anthropological and political implications of Kafka's work are most obvious in *The Penal Colony*. In the officer's report of the penal colony's past, the victim's torture and gradual transfiguration through dying figure as the ritual of a communal cult. Undoubtedly with anthropological discoveries in mind, Kafka presented the human scapegoat sacrificed for the benefit and edification of the community. On the other hand, the "brainwashing" of the subject, who is made to assent joyously to his own destruction, creates obvious parallels to the political and cultural irrationalism of the First World War (*The Penal Colony* was written two months after its outbreak) and the nascent totalitarianism that was to transform most of Europe into a huge penal colony less than three decades after Kafka had called his story as embarrassing "as our whole age."

At the same time, *The Penal Colony* illumines the autobiographical character of Kafka's whole work. No matter how interesting and fruitful the anthropological, sociological, and philosophical implications of Kafka's writings are—and they are considerable—the intimate autobiographical meaning must never be lost sight of, since it gives rise to and shapes all the rest. Kafka's greatness lay in his extraordinary ability to picture the universal in the intimate and the intimate in the universal. A multiplicity of referred meanings constitutes the powerful allusiveness and suggestiveness of every image he created. The communal festiveness that surrounds the dying prisoner in the penal colony provides the external correlative to the inner illumination he experiences. It also is an extension of the obviously personal conclusions of Georg Bendemann's and Gregor Samsa's lives. Georg Bendemann dies under a busy thoroughfare, in the center of city life, as it were. After his demise, Gregor Samsa becomes, for a while, the center of his family's hushed attention, a scenic arrangement, which anticipates the communal cult of death in *The Penal Colony* two years later.

As it systematizes in an image the whole first phase of Kafka's mature writing, the penal apparatus is also a metaphoric description of this writing itself. The machine transfigures and kills the prisoner literally by writing, by imprinting a sentence on the prisoner's flesh. The German word for "writing" (*Schrift*) which Kafka uses has the meaning of both "script" and "scripture," enabling Kafka to allude to the literary and religious significance of his penal apparatus at once. Above all, the machine repeats Kafka's own activity as a writer of punitive fantasies who grants his characters illuminating insights as he kills them.

In a diary entry of December 1914, Kafka shows that the penal apparatus is a pictorialized poetics of his writing. He confesses there that he savors in advance his own dying through the vicarious dying of his characters. Here Kafka attributes to himself the same attitude he depicts in the officer of the penal colony. The officer exults in the executions he arranges and supervises. He envies the beatitude his victims seem to attain and craves to take their place. However, when he finally does, the venerated machine merely "murders" him unceremoniously and instantly. No sign of inner illumination can be seen on him. The whole penal system is reduced to the officer's subjective assertion which his own execution contradicts. The objective truth is withheld.

This connects *The Penal Colony* with *The Trial*, which was begun a little over two months before the story and was left a fragment. Both Josef K., accused and executed without specified charge in the novel, and the officer in *The Penal Colony*, who executes himself to prove his claim for the penal machine and to savor the happiness he expects it to give, die a meaningless death. Punishment there is; but it no longer shows the truth. Thereby the two punitive fantasies of 1914 are profoundly different from those of two years before. This difference marks a turning point in Kafka's entire development. In *The Penal Colony* it is literally a change of perspective from the threatened façade to an inquiring objectivity. A detached observer—the explorer—listens to and then rejects the claims made for the punitive machine. Its subsequent collapse comes as the objective correlative of his rejection.

The perspective of *The Trial* is still that of a façade personality. There still is, as in the earlier punitive fantasies, a repressed past embodied in the protagonist's family, from which he has become estranged. However, the family is no longer central. An abstract authority, the Court, takes over the function of the accusing families of the earlier protagonists. It is no longer the intimate drama of father and son that shapes the narrative, but rather a conflict of principles.

Unlike the earlier punitive fantasies, *The Trial* does not specify the guilt for which its protagonist is arrested. The Court that judges Josef K. withholds the clear message given, in the earlier works, by father and family. Indeed, the confrontation of the self with its judge fails to take place. Punishment and annihilation remain; but understanding and atonement are gone.

The physical circumstances of Josef K.'s death reflect its subjective meaninglessness. Whereas Georg Bendemann dies in broad daylight, in the center of life, and Gregor Samsa departs with the first gleam of dawn, Josef K. is knifed in darkness and silence on the deserted periphery of his city. The external darkness surrounding him has its complement in the

[27]

darkness within him. He does not understand his death. As he fails to see his judges, so he fails to recognize himself. He does not discern within himself a conviction certain and firm enough to be his truth. His inner self remains as unfathomable as the Court.

The Trial is the only truly opaque work among the major writings of Kafka. Its opaqueness results from two factors: the total ambiguity of the Court and the total ambivalence of its hero.

If we understand that the Absolute had two distinct faces for Kafka, we shall do greater justice to his complexity than if we dismiss it as pure paradox. We might define these two aspects of the Absolute by attaching the name of Plato, a philosopher Kafka held in high esteem, to one and the name of Jehovah to the other. With its Platonic face, the Absolute was pure spirit and the physical world illusion; engagement in it was fatally wrong. With its other face—the face of Jehovah, behind whom the features of Kafka's robust and vital father lurked—it was energy and incessant will, a stream of generations and unending continuity of life. From this ambiguity within the Absolute, it followed that the self would become guilty in two opposite directions. It would become guilty before the Platonic aspect by getting "engaged," not merely sexually but economically and socially as well—by "wanting to snatch at the world with twenty hands," as Josef K. says of himself. On the other hand, the self would become guilty before the creator and progenitor of life by refusing "engagement" in the fullest sense of the word, by keeping itself pure in sterile virginity. In one case, it was the engaged and striving façade, in the other, the celibate true self that sinned and had to be sacrificed. The fate of Georg Bendemann shows the former, the fate of the misogynist officer of *The Penal Colony* or of the chaste sister of Barnabas in *The Castle* shows the latter guilt. *The Trial*, however, begun under the immediate shattering impact of Kafka's first break with his fiancée, Felice Bauer, illumines the double and, consequently, total guilt of the self. In Josef K.'s Court the two faces of the Absolute combine to form the enigmatic mask of total ambiguity.

There is a further reason for the novel's ambiguity. It is Josef K.'s inability to decide between the forces battling within him. In Josef K., an unacknowledged *homo religiosus* clashes with the consciousness of economic man. His official impulse of self-preservation and self-assertion resists the upsurge of his unofficial religious impulse, the craving for self-surrender and self-transcendence, objectified by his arrest. It is of highest significance that the Court comes closest to him and appeals to him most directly through a priest. The protagonists of *The Judgment* and *The Metamorphosis* were arrested by the submerged childhood of self within them. In Josef K. the submerged childhood of man, rather than of the individual, arrests the apparently emancipated façade of modern rationality.

By naming his protagonist Josef and adding the name Josef to the initial K. of his own name, Kafka might have hinted at this vertical split in himself and modern man. The "Josefstown" district of Prague, on the edge of which he had been born, had in his childhood still been the site of the ghetto and the center of criminal life. As he once remarked to Gustav Janouch, the new "Josefstown," with its broad streets and bright, airy buildings, presented only a "cover-up" surface, beneath which the dark, filthy, and frightful alleys of the ghetto lay merely submerged.

The careful reader becomes aware of this division within Josef K. Verbally, he seems to fight for reason, for man as defined by the rational legal system of the modern state, and denies the possibility of any extra-legal guilt. By his acts, however, he seeks out and, in the end, submits to the Court. In his mind he never comes to a clear decision for either one or the other. Consequently, the inner truth can never come to light. His conflicting pulls toward surrender, which would give meaning to his death, and toward resistance, which denies meaning to it, tear the whole concept of a true self apart. To be sure, the pull toward surrender and death does prove stronger. For K. lets himself be executed. He even awaits his executioners and leads them toward his place of execution. His consciousness, however, to the last, withholds definitive assent.

The total ambivalence of the hero becomes the total ambiguity of the story. To appreciate the full extent of this ambiguity, we merely have to compare the last thoughts of Georg Bendemann and Gregor Samsa with the last thought of Josef K. Their last thoughts express not only assent to their death but also affirmation and affection for life as embodied in their families. The last thought of *The Trial*, however, is "shame." Shame, it seems, will survive the protagonist. This final noun of the novel not only emphasizes a desperate negativity in contrast to the tragic affirmation with which the earlier punitive fantasies ended; it also expresses a total ambiguity, which makes it impossible to decipher the final meaning of *The Trial*. For it is entirely uncertain to what the noun "shame" refers. It could refer to Josef K.'s failure to resist his execution, or to the senselessness of his murder, and to the shamefulness of a court that orders such injustices. In either case, "shame" would express Josef K.'s mental defiance coexisting with his physical submission. However, it could also refer to his refusal to kill himself or to understand what the Court expects of him. Then the novel would have the opposite meaning. Josef K. would be justly punished for his stubborn rejection of the possibility of his guilt. Both in-

[30]

terpretations are equally justified even though contrary to each other. The unrelieved ambiguity of *The Trial* dissolves, therefore, not only the idea of a true self but also the possibility of discerning a truth altogether.

This ambiguity of the work reflects not only the ambivalence of the character but also the ambivalence of the author. In its last thought the consciousness of the character has become the comment of the narrator. It was Kafka himself who could not come to a decision about the meaning of his novel. He excised passages that would have shown Josef K.'s craving to be united with the Court or his longing to be transfigured in death, and would have made him resemble the officer of *The Penal Colony*. Kafka crossed out a reverie of Josef K. which would have been the opposite of his actual death in the novel's final scene. In that passage Josef K. succeeds in entering the court house whence the warrant of his arrest had been issued, and he experiences a transfiguration, symbolized by a new garment of perfect fit. By eliminating this radiant vision from the novel, that is, from the consciousness of his protagonist, Kafka himself enacted the process of repression which his hero is engaged in. Josef K. exhibits tendencies toward surrender and suicide which form the powerful subterranean drift that counteracts his ever conscious intention and action and pulls him ever further along toward destruction. These persist subliminally in fleeting thoughts, gestures, and unreasoned acts, to which Josef K. seems to be driven. Except for the initial arrest, it is always Josef K. who either actively seeks or welcomes contact with the Court. Josef K.'s longing for contact with the Court emerges perhaps most clearly in the Titorelli chapter. Josef K. rejects the painter's suggestions for compromise solutions and insists on absolute acquittal by the highest Judges. His insistence amounts to a full recognition of their supreme authority over him and, beyond that, implies his wish to be accepted and approved by them. This is the limit to which Kafka allows K.'s wish for the Court to become conscious.

In his preceding works Kafka revealed the strategies of repression his heroes engaged in and let the truth be said. In writing *The Trial* he imitated his character and threw out anything that might reveal him directly and unambiguously. In the process of creating his protagonist, Kafka himself performed the activity that constituted his character. He excised and refused to show the "whole truth." Consequently he expunged dreams that would have betrayed Josef K. to himself and to the reader. In *The Castle*, where he deals with a hero much more conscious of his purposes, Kafka leaves K.'s dream in the text and also allows him a revealing childhood memory.

The reasons for Kafka's excisions in *The Trial* are twofold. For one thing they show that he desired to make so complete the division between the conscious surface and the subterranean level in his protagonist's character that Josef K. would be utterly unaware of one level of himself and the reader would be unaware of what compelled Josef K. toward his destruction. Josef K. thus became the precise image of the modern Central European bourgeois who, in our century, would be caught unawares by the eruption of destructive irrationalism around him; yet the tendencies that made this possible were to be found within the bourgeois himself. In this respect Kafka's own art did what he ascribed to the art of Picasso: it portrayed the distortions of reality that had not yet entered consciousness. Secondly Kafka, at the stage of *The Trial*, could no longer bring himself to condone his hero's conscious assent to the judgment that would destroy him.

There is one part of the novel, however, in which the other side of Josef K., which the author elsewhere excludes from

[32]

the explicit text of the novel, is openly shown. This is the parable, "Before the Law," which the prison chaplain tells to Josef K. in the cathedral chapter. Here the radiance that streams from the Court in Josef K.'s repressed dream is allowed to shine forth openly, and the man from the country, who seeks entrance into the Law, is allowed to express freely what Josef K., who thinks of himself as a modern, rational man, can never bring himself to acknowledge: that the desire for union with the mystic Law is the fundamental concern of his existence.

The parable, or "legend," as Kafka himself called it, "Before the Law," presents the split within Josef K. as an explicit coexistence between desire and fear. The man from the country came to join the Law but is prevented by the doorkeeper, who tells him he cannot let him enter now. He adds that the man might try to go in, but he frightens him with the prospect of more dreadful doorkeepers farther along.

The Law thus presents an ambiguity which the man had not expected. He had thought of it only as highly desirable and enticing. Now it also shows a threatening face. It seems that this ambiguity of the Law offers the key to the parable. This is true, if we restrict ourselves to the perspective of the man. However, as we shall see, here, in the second phase of Kafka's maturity, the perspective of the protagonist is not the perspective of the narrative. For a narrator has been put between reader and protagonist. If we see the man from the perspective of the narrator, we find that the ambiguity of the Law is a tool and catalyst for making the man's ambivalence his destiny. For the ambiguity, introduced by the doorkeeper, merely brings out an ambivalence within the man. His desire for the Law is now complicated by his fear of it. Desire and fear begin to exist side by side in the man.

What connects him with Josef K., and makes his destiny a

[33]

perfect illustration of the novel, is his inability to opt for either side of his ambivalence. What he decides is to yield to his fear without giving up his desire. He defers his entrance and begins to wait before the door to the Law. He chooses a life of ambivalance. The consequences of his choice are degradation and lifelong frustration. He is literally lowered, by having to spend his life crouching on a footstool at the feet of the forbidding sentry. He is morally degraded by resorting to bribery and cajolery, and he is intellectually reduced to begging the fleas in the doorkeeper's collar to intercede for him. In the end he dies without having attained his goal.

The relationship of this parable to the novel in which it was originally written illustrates very well the different narrative principle of the second phase of Kafka's maturity. The rest of the novel was composed before the parable and indeed before *Penal Colony*. Both parabolic stories helped Kafka to clarify the problem of his novel. What the parable "Before the Law" accomplishes is to illuminate the basic problem of Josef K., his paralyzing ambivalence. In the narrative form of Kafka's punitive fantasies, which used the perspective of the façade, this ambivalence could not be clarified since it could not enter the conscious level of the narrative; Josef K.'s proud rationality, his façade, could not permit his longing for the Court to show itself openly at any time. In the parable, however, there is no façade, and the two conflicting forces within man are clearly presented as existing side by side. In place of the vertical division of layers, which we have found in the punitive fantasies, there is again the horizontal split which we found in Raban's wish dream, but now it is without the separation of façade and true self.

The man from the country is Josef K.'s repressed truth exposed to view. This emerges clearly from the fact that Josef K., when he hears the parable, spontaneously identifies with the man from the country. Josef K. shares with the subject of the parable an ambivalence of desire and fear. Unlike Josef K., however, the man from the country does not repress his desire; he merely defers it. In contrast to the opaqueness of Josef K.'s fate, the parable, therefore, makes transparent the fatal incompatibility of man's desire for union with the Absolute and his fear for life and safety. By its transparency, the parabolic form, which characterizes Kafka's second phase, goes even further in elucidating the problem it presents. The parable "Before the Law" implies quite clearly that the man from the country could find a "way out" of his impasse by abandoning his fear and entering the gate regardless of the risks awaiting him; if he were to choose to go forward, despite the injunctions of the doorkeeper, he would attain true self-fulfillment. However, the man in the parable could also do the opposite; he could yield to his fear and abandon his desire, leave the gate and turn his back forever on doorkeeper and Law. Such a retreat would amount to an abandonment of self, insofar as his self is identical with its dominant concern. By the same token, it would assure not only his physical survival—that he insures anyway by choosing not to go into the Law—but also a survival in dignity and independence. He would gain a life emancipated from obsession.

The choice open to the man in the priest's parable defines the problem around which Kafka's subsequent work revolves. In his second and third phase Kafka no longer describes the catastrophic eruption of a hidden truth and the resultant destruction of his protagonist; instead he presents a dilemma attendant upon his protagonist's attempt to realize his true self which would, at the same time, be a union with or recognition by a higher power, authority, or collective. In Kafka's late work the self of his protagonist is undivided and openly dedicated to its craving or quest. The conflict is not between

[35]

a façade and a true self, but between the true self and an external power that disavows the self's claims or frustrates its expectations. Like the Law in the "legend," the external power in Kafka's later works both beckons and forbids entrance to itself. Between the protagonist's imaginings and the behavior of external reality there exists a discrepancy which is the subject of the self's reflections and comments. The protagonist hopes that somehow the contradiction will be resolved. He hopes that reality will conform eventually to his expectations; this hope constitutes his true self and is the mission to which he subordinates and for which he utilizes everything. If he were to give up his hope, he would have to renounce his self and nature, as the ape does in "A Report to an Academy." All other characters of Kafka's later work, clinging to their missions, are yet unable to change reality and influence it according to their desire. They spend their lives waiting in front of closed entrances, locked out from the goal they crave. Indeed, the title of Kafka's last and greatest novel, *The Castle* (*Das Schloss*, 1922), a marvelous elaboration and development of the theme of the "legend" "Before the Law," carries in German the subsidiary meaning of "lock." For K. the castle is literally a lock that locks him out. Unable to gain the entrance and likewise unable to resign and turn their backs on it, the protagonists of Kafka's late works stay doggedly loyal and true to their quest. But their loyalty or stubbornness immobilizes them. They waste their lives in visible or invisible cages, prisons of their own devising.

Cage, castle or "lock," underground fortress or burrow are dominant images of Kafka's last works. At the end of his second phase, he presents the image of the cage in "A Report," concluding the volume of parables which "Before the Law" initiated chronologically; and the cage appears again in "A Hunger Artist," title story of his last volume of narratives. The

[36]

two stories are contrasting approaches to the theme of the cage. We have already drawn attention to the solution of the captured ape who cannot stand life in the cage and finds a "way out" by ceasing to be what he is and becoming something else. The hunger artist takes the opposite course. He voluntarily enters and stays in the cage in order to express his true self.

The hunger artist's wish to be recognized as the incomparable artist he is, is not fulfilled; the public first misunderstands, then neglects and ignores him. Looking at the narrative through the protagonist's perspective, we are inclined to accuse the public of callousness, vulgarity, and cruelty. Similarly, seeing through Josef K.'s perspective in the cathedral chapter of *The Trial*, we are inclined to blame the doorkeeper for keeping the man out of the law. However, Kafka underwent a great change toward analytic clarity and explicitness in the near-decade after he wrote the "legend." If we understand the story "A Hunger Artist" as an indictment of the public, Kafka's text convicts us of being wrong. For, at the end of his life, the hunger artist informs the world explicitly that he deserves no admiration. He had been a sport of nature, a freak, unable to find food that satisfied him, and, therefore, incapable of doing anything else but starve. If he had found food to his taste, he would have eaten like everyone else and led a completely undistinguished life.

Like the punitive fantasies, "A Hunger Artist" presents a discrepancy between the official perspective of the story—given by the protagonist—and the truth. The perspective of the punitive fantasies, seeing the protagonists as victims of external injustice and outrageous fortune, tends to prevent us from noting the submerged inner force that drives them to their catastrophes. Similarly, the hunger artist's perspective makes us sympathize with him as the victim of the public and

[37]

overlook the crucial fact that his exhibition is a fraud. For he makes us accept something as admirable achievement that, as he himself admits in the end, is nothing more than a necessity and, indeed, a debility, for which pity rather than admiration might be the proper response. Knowing his natural defect, the hunger artist should not have expected admiring recognition; but he made us—the readers—believe that this was his due.

In Kafka's final phase we return to the deviousness and deceptiveness of a perspective that distorts and conceals the truth of the story, and is defeated by it. Again the protagonist's claim and grievance against the world are unjustified; they are deceit. His frustration and final refutation or capitulation reveal the truth. As in the punitive fantasies, it is in the dying of the self through which truth conquers and shines forth. Dying, the hunger artist unmasks the fraud his life had been. Like Gregor Samsa, with whom many analogies connect him, he finds in death the contentment that life had consistently denied him.

Yet there is an essential difference between the punitive fantasies and Kafka's final phase. The punitive fantasies unveiled a contrast between the façade and the truth of the self. The late works oppose a unified self to truth. The hunger artist's self is not divided between façade and true self. On the contrary, his mission, symbolized by the cage in which it takes place, is the uncompromising and absolute expression of his true and only self. His starving is the full revelation of his inner truth.

However, this inner truth is, in itself, a deception. Herein lies the paradox of Kafka's last phase. In it the self is a pretense and presumption. The hunger artist's complete ' otherness," his inability to eat and, therefore, be like other men, would in itself not be a fraud but a mere eccentricity that would exclude him from humanity. The hunger artist, however, refuses to stay outside humanity. This refusal drives him to proclaim as art the defect with which he was born and exhibit it for public acclaim. Art and fraud are inseparable in him. For he is an artist only by virtue of committing his fraud, or, put differently, his decision to treat his natural want as though it were a skill makes him artist and fraud at the same time. It is this decision that makes him enter the cage. The cage exhibits both untruth and art, yet it also symbolizes absolute subjectively and otherness. No one but he can fast indefinitely; no one resembles him. His isolated existence in the cage dooms any hope for true appreciation and understanding from the public beyond his bars. For he is on exhibit as a freak. His "art" or, more truly said, his nature is unique—so subjective, so different from the interests and feelings of other men that the hunger artist's monstrous spirituality cannot possibly be more than a short-lived sensation in the life of mankind.

Whereas the hunger artist makes his fraud explicit, the immense deception perpetrated by the Land Surveyor K. in *The Castle* is never stated explicitly, and K. has, therefore, fooled most readers, critics, and exegetes of the novel. K. claims to have been called and appointed land surveyor by the castle which controls the village into which he has strayed one night. He makes us believe that the castle authorities, by refusing to honor his claim, treat him unjustly and deprive him of what by right is his. He presses his claim with such urgency and consistency that the reader feels compelled to accept it at face value and to see in K. a victim of soulless bureaucracy or to construct elaborate schemes of interpretation based on the "injustice" done to K. Consequently, *The Castle* appeared in critical literature as a satire on bureaucracy, an adumbration of totalitarianism, an allegory of social injustice or of the religious problem of man's insistence on justice and God's grace. All these interpretations are the result of the critics' being duped by K.'s colossal fraud. A close reading of the text reveals that K. has no legitimate claim on the Castle because he never was appointed land surveyor. This truth of the novel is revealed by inconsistencies in the plot and by a brief passage of K.'s inner monologue. These allow only one conclusion: K. had never been called by the Castle.

K. has no document to prove his call. He promises, however, that his assistants will soon arrive with his apparatus. They never come. Instead K. is given two new "assistants" by the Castle. These assistants know nothing about land surveying and have no apparatus. K. has never seen them before. Thus the "proof" of K.'s appointment, which the promised arrival of his old assistants and apparatus was supposed to be, never materializes. The fact that K. accepts his new assistants without waiting for his old assistants or ever thinking of them shows that, in all likelihood, they do not exist.

A telephone inquiry at the Castle produces the answer that nothing is known of K.'s appointment. Immediately thereafter, a call from the Castle reverses this first answer and confirms K.'s claim. K.'s mental reaction to this information unmasks him as an imposter. Instead of registering with simple satisfaction the news that the "misunderstanding" has been cleared up, K. considers the Castle's recognition of his claim "unpropitious." He takes it to be a "smiling acceptance" of his "challenge," designed to "cow him" by "lofty superiority." The term "challenge," used by K. in this context, shows that he does not expect to step into a promised position but that he comes with the purpose of fighting the Castle and forcing it to yield something to him, either the coveted office or something else. It is clear that he was never appointed land surveyor and called to the Castle. He is a stranger who, for reasons which we shall examine, "challenges" the Castle to submit to his unfounded claim. The Castle seems to "accept" his "challenge" and plays a game with him which forms the plot of the novel.

This close reading of the text alters the whole basis of interpretation of Kafka's last and greatest novel. It can no longer be maintained that the conflict between justice and injustice, no matter on what level, is its theme. Its theme is rather K.'s attempt to make everyone, including the reader, believe that justice is the problem and that the injustice inflicted upon him is his motive in his struggle with the Castle. Kafka has K. conduct his campaign so skillfully and emphatically that he persuades most readers to believe him, contrary to the textual evidence he himself provides. In his richest and most profound work Kafka depicts the victory of fiction over reality. The deception perpetrated by his character triumphs not over the other characters—for no one in the novel really believes K.— but over the reader.

Kafka achieves this amazing triumph of art by the masterful application of a narrative perspective which misleads the reader into mistaking the protagonist's view for the truth. However, while creating this victory of fiction, Kafka at the same time exposes its falseness through his protagonist's own oblique self-revelations. Furthermore, the fact that the hero's claim never attains true recognition in the novel shows its vanity. In a letter to Max Brod, written in the year 1922, at the time of *The Castle*'s composition, Kafka defined the writer's essence as "vanity." Kafka's late work, especially his artist stories, "A Hunger Artist" and "Josephine," shows vanity both as narcissism and as futility. It shows that the attempt of subjectivity to impose its terms upon external reality must always fail.

The Castle answers K.'s attack with an ironically exact retribution. It meets his unreal claim by an equally unreal ap-

[41]

pointment. Klamm's letter appoints K. as Land Surveyor, and he will henceforth be addressed as such; but he obtains no land to survey and is never established in an appropriate office. The title given him by the Castle is as gratuitous and empty as his pretended call. The Castle gives him assistants who are irrelevant to his professed profession. They can assist him in his land surveying as little as can the instruments he claims he has but is unable to produce. These assistants also cause him to do to them what he claims the Castle has done to him. As the Castle locks him out and will not admit him, he locks out his assistants and refuses to let them come to him. K. himself displays the cruelty and injustice he ascribes to the Castle. Moreover, even as he took his mistress away from Klamm, his own chief, so he loses her again to one of his assistants. In this late work judgment appears not as destruction, but as ironic retribution.

The Castle counters K.'s maneuver by presenting a universe in which there is no certainty and nothing is what it seems to be. This is the necessary consequence of the fact that the protagonist, too, is not what he seems to be. That is, K.'s self is not a fact but a pretense. It is a desperate experiment, an attempt to impose his fiction upon the reality that confronts and excludes him. He needs this fiction to break into and become part of the reality he faces.

Kafka, in *The Castle*, describes the fundamental situation of modern man, for whom neither the world nor his own self is given and certain. Like every man, K., in order to be, has to be recognized and related as an individual to the whole of society; he must have a specific calling. In order to get his call, he must already be someone, an accredited and required expert. However, K. knows he has no call and is, therefore, nothing. He is a stranger, utterly unconnected, and superfluous—locked out by the *Schloss* functioning in its basic meaning of "lock." Since a human being cannot live permanently outside humanity, K. desperately needs to enter it, that is, to become someone needed and recognized. In order to live, he has to "unlock" the lock with which humanity excludes him. As the dominant necessity of life and the essence of desirability, *"das Schloss"* presents to him its other meaning in the guise of the magically beckoning and unattainable castle. It is K.'s staggering and superhuman task to create the call he needs. He has to pretend that he already possesses what he has come to get— the necessary prerequisite for beginning an integrated and authentic existence. Therefore, his battle with the Castle is not a whim but a desperate necessity. Precisely because he has no objectively valid claim for recognition, he must force the Castle to honor his subjective pretense—his fiction—as the truth. K. fights to become in truth what he pretends he is— the land surveyor called by the Castle.

K.'s quest is a metaphoric statement of the lifelong struggle which Kafka's entire writing sought to describe. (Significantly, his first work bears the title "Description of a Struggle.") At the time he composed *The Castle* Kafka wrote to his woman friend and lover, Milena, that he was given nothing, that he must create not only his present and his future but his past as well. His task is, therefore, infinitely more difficult than that of other men. For not only must he fight the battle for his future that every man has to wage but, while engaged in that battle, he must also be acquiring a past, a ground on which he can stand and all others can take for granted as their birthright and inheritance.

Kafka related this peculiar predicament to the fate of the Westernized Jew in Europe who, already uprooted and cut off from his ancestral traditions, is not yet permitted to enter fully and truly the life of his hosts. Beyond this personal and national meaning, however, Kafka presents in *The Castle* the task facing modern man in general. Unmoored from his spiritual and social anchorage, expelled from his once secure place in the cosmos, modern man, as the Existentialists point out, has to make his own identity and project his own existence instead of assuming it as given. Kafka's fragmentary novel depicts the tragic irony and ultimate impossibility of this enterprise.

SELECTED BIBLIOGRAPHY

NOTE: *The first edition of Kafka's Collected Writings appeared, edited by Max Brod, in Berlin and Prague, in 1935–1937. It included the first five volumes listed below. It was revised and reissued by Schocken Books in New York in 1946. This edition still forms the standard edition of Kafka's works in German. Subsequent volumes, edited by Max Brod and, in one case, Willy Haas, were added, as listed below. All were published by Schocken Books in New York.*

PRINCIPAL WORKS OF FRANZ KAFKA

Vol. 1. Erzählungen and kleine Prosa. (This volume contains all works published by Kafka himself in his lifetime.)
Vol. 2. Amerika.
Vol. 3. Der Prozess.
Vol. 4. Das Schloss.
Vol. 5. Beschreibung eines Kampfes. Novellen, Skizzen, Aphorismen aus dem Nachlass.
    Tagebücher. 1910–1923. 1948 and 1949.
    Hochzeitsvorbereitungen auf dem Lande und andere Prosa aus dem Nachlass. 1953.
    Briefe. 1958.
    Briefe an Milena. Edited by Willy Haas. 1952.

PRINCIPAL TRANSLATIONS OF KAFKA'S WORKS

The Penal Colony. Stories and Short Pieces. Translated by Willa and Edwin Muir. New York, Schocken Books, 1948. (Paperback edition 1961.) (This volume represents the translation of Volume I of the German edition of Kafka's Collected Writings.)
Amerika. Translated by Edwin Muir. Preface by Klaus Mann. Afterword by Max Brod. New York, New Directions, 1940. (Paperback edition 1962.)
Amerika. A Novel. Translated by Willa and Edwin Muir. New York, Schocken Books, 1962. Paperback.

The Trial. Definitive edition. Translated by Willa and Edwin Muir.
Revised, and with additional materials translated by E. M. Butler.
New York, Alfred A. Knopf, 1957. (First edition 1937.)

The Castle. Definitive edition. Translated by Willa and Edwin
Muir, with additional material translated by Eithne Wilkins and
Ernst Kaiser, with a homage by Thomas Mann. New York, Al-
fred A. Knopf, 1954. (Reissued 1964. First edition 1930.)

Selected Short Stories of Franz Kafka. Translated by Willa and
Edwin Muir. Introduced by Philip Rahv. New York, The Modern Library, Random House, 1952.

The Great Wall of China. Stories and Reflections. Translated by
Willa and Edwin Muir. New York, Schocken Books, 1946.
(Fourth printing 1960.)

Dearest Father. Stories and Other Writings. Translated by Ernst
Kaiser and Eithne Wilkins. New York, Schocken Books, 1954.

Description of a Struggle. Translated by Tania and James Stern.
New York, Schocken Books, 1958.

Parables and Paradoxes. Bilingual. German and English. New York,
Schocken Books, 1962. Paperback. (First edition was called
Parables and was published in 1947.)

The Diaries of Franz Kafka. 1910–1913. Edited by Max Brod.
Translated by Joseph Kresh. New York, Schocken Books, 1948.
(Paperback edition 1965.) (First edition 1947.)

The Diaries of Franz Kafka. 1914–1923. Edited by Max Brod.
Translated by Martin Greenberg, with the co-operation of
Hannah Arendt. New York, Schocken Books, 1949. (Paperback
edition 1965.)

Letters to Milena. Edited by Willi Haas. Translated by Tania and
James Stern. New York, Schocken Books, 1953. (Paperback
edition 1962.)

BIOGRAPHICAL AND CRITICAL LITERATURE ON KAFKA

Anders, Günther. Franz Kafka. Pro und contra. Munich, C. H.
Beck, 1951.

———— Franz Kafka. Translated by A. Steer and A. K. Thorlby.
New York, Hillary House Publishers, 1960.

Arendt, Hannah. "Franz Kafka. A Revaluation," *Partisan Review*,
XI (1944), 412–22.

Beissner, Friedrich. Der Erzähler Franz Kafka. Ein Vortrag. Stuttgart, Kohlhammer, 1952.

Brod, Max, Franz Kafka. Eine Biographie. Dritte, erweiterte Auflage. New York, Schocken Books, 1954. (First edition 1937.)
—— Franz Kafka. A Biography. Translated by G. Humphreys Roberts and Richard Winston. Second, enlarged edition. New York, Schocken Books, 1960.

✳ Camus, Albert. "Hope and the Absurd in the Work of Franz Kafka," in The Myth of Sisyphus and Other Essays. Translated from the French by Justin O'Brien. New York, Alfred A. Knopf, 1955, 124–38. (Paperback edition Vintage Books, n.d., 92–102. Original French edition Paris, Gallimard, 1943.)

Dentan, Michel. Humour et création littéraire dans l'oeuvre de Kafka. Geneva, Droz, 1961.

Eisner, Pavel. Franz Kafka and Prague. Translated by Lowry Nelson and René Wellek. New York, Arts Inc., 1950.

Emrich, Wilhelm. Franz Kafka. Bonn, Anthenäum, 1958.

Flores, Angel (editor). The Kafka Problem. New York, New Directions, 1946. (Reissued New York, Octagon Books, n.d.)
—— and Homer Swander (editors). Franz Kafka Today. Madison, The University of Wisconsin Press, 1958.

Gray, Ronald. Kafka's Castle. Cambridge, The University Press, 1956.
—— (editor). Kafka. A Collection of Critical Essays. Englewood Cliffs, N.J., Prentice-Hall, 1963. (Kafka. Twentieth-Century Views. Spectrum Books. Prentice-Hall.)

Janouch, Gustav. Gespräche mit Kafka. Erinnerungen und Aufzeichnungen. Frankfurt am Main, Fischer, 1951.
—— Conversations with Kafka. Notes and Reminiscences, with an introduction by Max Brod. Translated by Goronwy Rees. New York, F.A. Praeger, 1953.

Järv, Harry. Die Kafka-Literatur. Eine Bibliographie. Malmö, Lund, Cavefors, 1961.

Martini, Fritz. "Franz Kafka. Das Schloss," in Das Wagnis der Sprache. Interpretationen deutscher Prosa von Nietzsche bis Benn. Stuttgart, Ernst Klett Verlag, 1956, pp. 287–335. (First edition 1954.)

Neider, Charles. The Frozen Sea. A Study of Franz Kafka. New York, Russell and Russell, 1962. (First edition New York, Oxford University Press, 1948.)

Politzer, Heinz. Franz Kafka. Parable and Paradox. Ithaca, New York, Cornell University Press, 1962.

Robert, Marthe. Kafka. Paris, Gallimard, 1960.

Sarraute, Natalie. L'ère du soupçon. Essais sur le roman. Paris, Gallimard, 1956.

[47]

Slochower, Harry, ed. A Franz Kafka Miscellany. Rev. enlarged second edition. New York, The Twice a Year Press, 1946. (First edition 1940.)

Sokel, Walter H. Franz Kafka. Tragik und Ironie. Zur Struktur seiner Kunst. Munich and Vienna, Albert Langen-Georg Müller, 1964.

Spann, Meno. "The Minor Kafka Problem," *The Germanic Review*, XXXII (1957), 163–77.

Spilka, Mark. Dickens and Kafka. A Mutual Interpretation. Bloomington, Indiana University Press, 1963.

Tauber, Herbert. Franz Kafka. An Interpretation of his Works. Translated by G. Humphreys Roberts and Roger Senhouse. New Haven, Yale University Press, 1948.

Wagenbach, Klaus. Franz Kafka. Eine Biographie seiner Jugend. 1883–1912. Bern, Francke, 1958.

4